SOCCER

Junior Sports

Morgan Hughes

Rourke
Publishing LLC
Vero Beach, Florida 32964

www.rourkepublishing.com

PHOTO CREDITS: Cover, title page, p 5, 6, 11, 13, 15, 20, 26, 28, 29 Photos.com; p 9 Simon Bruty/Getty; p 12 Stanley Chou/Getty; p 16 Franck Fife/Getty; p 18 David Cannon/Getty; p 19 Paolo Cocco/Getty; p 22, 23 Clipart.com; p 25 J-C Verhaegen/Getty

Title page: *Good footwork is the key to being a successful soccer player.*

Editor: Frank Sloan

Library of Congress Cataloging-in-Publication Data

Hughes, Morgan, 1957-
  Soccer / Morgan Hughes.
     p. cm. -- (Junior sports)
  Includes bibliographical references and index.
  ISBN 1-59515-187-7 (hardcover)
  1. Soccer--Juvenile literature. I. Title. II. Series: Hughes, Morgan, 1957-   Junior sports.
  GV943.25.H84 2004
  796.334--dc22
                                    2004009367

Printed in the USA

CG/CG

TABLE OF CONTENTS

The Basics 4
The Gear 8
Kicking 10
Dribbling 14
Passing 17
Trapping 21
Goalkeeping 24
Special Kicks 27
Glossary 30
Further Reading/Websites 31
Index 32

THE BASICS

Soccer is one of the most popular participation sports for athletes of all ages the world over. The international name for soccer is football—though it in no way resembles American football. The sport got its start in England and Scotland in the 1800s. Today more boys and girls in the United States play soccer than any other single sport.

Soccer is played everywhere in the world, as this shot of fans in a giant stadium shows.

A standard soccer field (or pitch) is 110 to 120 yards (100.5 to 109.7 m) long and 70 to 80 yards (64 to 73.1 m) wide. Permanent lines mark the space in front of each goal—the goal areas. Larger rectangles outside these goal areas are called the penalty areas.

Soccer builds leadership skills, encourages teamwork, and puts smiles on faces.

Each team typically fields 11 players. In a standard 4-3-3 formation, there are four defensive backfielders, three midfielders, and three strikers, plus the goalkeeper.

The game is played in two 45-minute halves of running time—the clock does not stop when play is halted. The referee may add time at the end of each half to make up for delays if players are injured.

Some historians say the word "soccer" came from English schoolboy slang. From a nod to Association Football, the word "association" became "assoc" then took the slang "er" ending.

THE GEAR

Soccer can be played informally with almost no special equipment. The modern soccer ball is constructed of **synthetic** materials and is light and lasts a long time. At more organized levels, players wear cleated (spiked) shoes for better footing and plastic guards to protect the shins.

Soccer balls from the late 19th century were made of leather panels and were so heavy that "heading" the ball could cause serious injury.

With the extra grip that cleats provide you'll be better able to turn and keep your footing at high speed.

KICKING

The key to moving the ball in soccer is proper footwork, or kicking. Players use both feet and the front and both sides of each foot to direct the ball and to apply spin when shooting or passing.

Good balance is **fundamental** to successful footwork. This is partly achieved by keeping the head still when kicking. Strong legs are another must for any serious soccer player. Running, biking, stair climbing, and jogging all contribute to building strong legs.

Unlike tackling in American football, which requires actual physical contact, tackling in soccer means taking the ball from an opponent *without* physical contact.

Kicking the ball takes more than just your foot. Strength comes from the entire leg, as well as from proper body rotation.

The striking point for kicking the ball is the top (instep) of the foot—not the toes. Imagine kicking with the laces of your shoes. Whether shooting or passing to a teammate, try to place the non-kicking foot beside the ball to avoid hitting too far in front of or behind the ball.

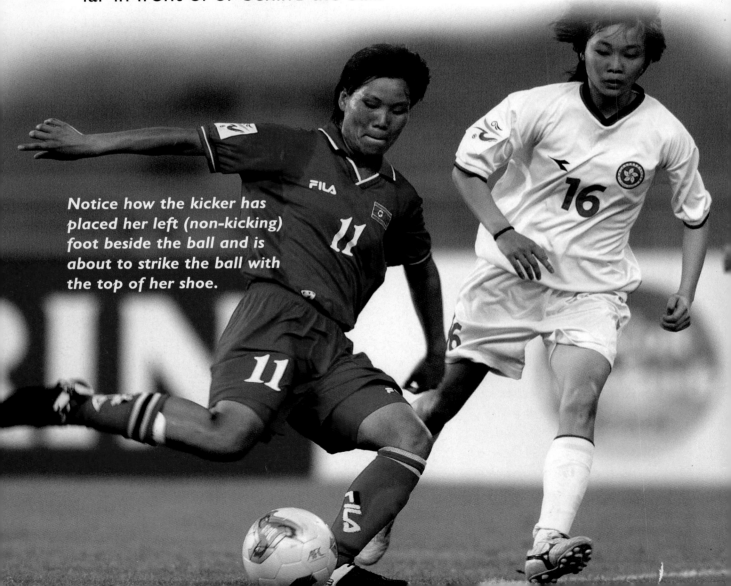

Notice how the kicker has placed her left (non-kicking) foot beside the ball and is about to strike the ball with the top of her shoe.

One of the most exciting—and difficult—kicks in soccer is the bicycle kick. This is typically **executed** by a striker very near the opponents' goal. With his or her back to the goal, the shooter must throw his or her legs high into the air and kick the ball while falling backward—and then land safely.

Done successfully, the bicycle kick can catch even the best goalie off-guard.

DRIBBLING

Dribbling is the fine art of controlling the ball at any speed while a defender tries to take it away from you. Dribbling is used in soccer—just as it is in basketball—to move the ball around the field of play. Soccer players may not use their hands, however, only their feet.

Learning to dribble with confidence can be a difficult and time-consuming exercise. It can also make the difference between a good and an excellent soccer player. Speed and agility will come with practice. Just remember: keep the ball as close to your feet as possible.

When you practice your dribbling skills, do it at a pace that feels as close to game speed as possible.

PASSING

Next to **honing** skills as a shooter, no weapon serves the soccer player better than the art of passing the ball. This requires not only physical ability but also a keen awareness of the field. Above all else, soccer is a team sport. A team-first attitude among all players is a must.

When dribbling, it's important to keep your head up so you can see the field. When making a pass, however, be sure you watch the ball leave your foot.

Many sports experts agree that the best thing about any team sport isn't the winning but the friends you make along the way.

Since soccer is a running game, practice passing the ball to moving objects rather than **stationary** ones. A good passer not only puts the ball in the area where a teammate is currently stationed, but also leads that teammate to a spot where he or she is about to arrive.

Speed is important, but so is concentrating on the ball.

You cannot use your hands to make a pass. However, it is perfectly acceptable, once you master the skill, to use your head to redirect the ball.

To give or receive a pass, you need to get body position against your opponent.

Trapping is a good way to control the ball, particularly when an opponent is right on top of you trying the get the ball away.

TRAPPING

There are two ends to every pass: the sender and the receiver. Since you can't use your hands to catch the ball, trapping it is the next best thing. This is done by clamping one foot down on the top of the ball as it arrives, damping its energy before it bounces away.

If you're positioned in such a way that the ball arrives at an angle, use either the inside or outside of your foot to trap the ball against the ground. In all cases, this **maneuver** should be done quickly and smoothly. This will allow the flow of play to continue and help you avoid tacklers.

On long airborne passes, players may also use their chests to "catch" the ball. This **technique** requires good coordination and body control.

Although opponents can't physically put hands on you, they're free to kick at the ball, so use body position to protect it.

Being in the right place at the right time will make you an even more effective player.

GOALKEEPING

No player is more in the spotlight than the goalkeeper. As the last line of defense, the goalie's mistakes can turn the tide of a game. Standing before the gaping 8-by-24-foot- (2.4-by-7.3-m-) goal cage, even the most gifted keeper can feel small and **vulnerable**.

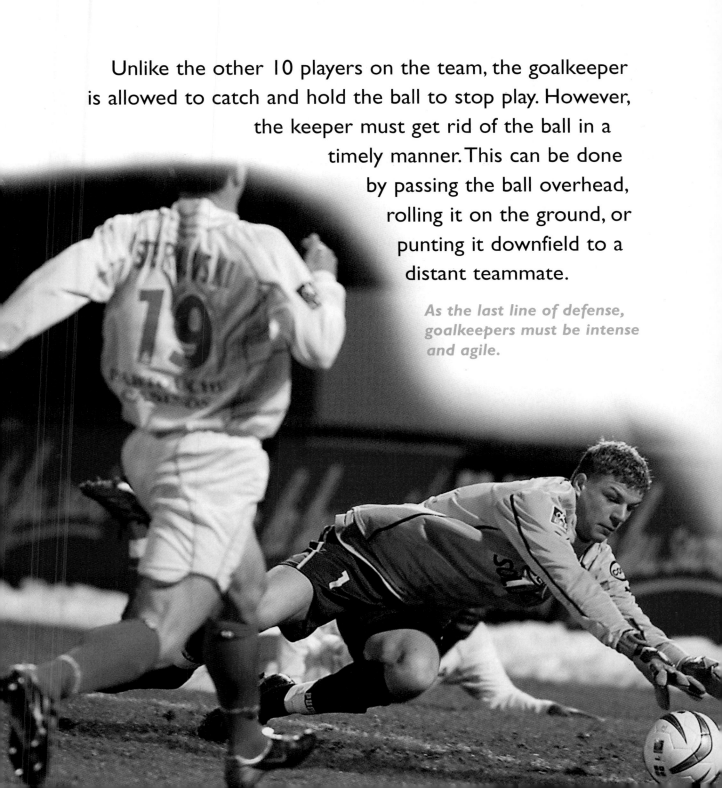

Unlike the other 10 players on the team, the goalkeeper is allowed to catch and hold the ball to stop play. However, the keeper must get rid of the ball in a timely manner. This can be done by passing the ball overhead, rolling it on the ground, or punting it downfield to a distant teammate.

As the last line of defense, goalkeepers must be intense and agile.

Goalkeepers wear a different color jersey from those worn by their teammates. This is so the referee can easily determine in a scramble who is handling the ball. The goalie may also wear specially designed gloves to avoid broken fingers as well as to increase grip on the ball.

Goalkeepers sometimes resemble acrobats with the amazing saves they make.

SPECIAL KICKS

Penalty kicks are awarded if a defender in the 18-foot-(5.5-m-) box in front of his own goal commits a foul (e.g., pushing, tripping). The offended team chooses a player to attempt the kick, which is then made from the spot of the foul with only the goalkeeper to beat.

For all its non-stop action and high level of skill, soccer is one of the lowest scoring games in the world. Goals are extremely important.

Like a penalty kick, a free kick is awarded after a foul. The free kick may either be direct (a shot on goal) or indirect (it must touch two players before a shot on goal is taken). In either case, the defending team retreats 10 yards (9.1 m) from the point of the kick.

The goalkeeper is a very lonely figure when facing a penalty kick.

The corner kick is awarded when the defending team puts the ball out of bounds behind its own goal. The ball is placed in the triangle in the appropriate corner of the field. A player adept at slicing or arcing the ball has a pretty good chance at scoring on a corner kick. The corner kick is an exciting moment in any soccer match, with a goal—or even the final score—on the line.

Each of the four corners of the soccer pitch has a painted triangle. This is where the ball is placed for a corner kick.

GLOSSARY

executed (EX eh KYOO ted) — carried out, put into effect, performed

fundamental (fun da MEN tal) — a basic, essential element

honing (HONE ing) — perfecting or making more intense, sharpening

maneuver (mah NOO ver) — a physical movement requiring skill or dexterity

stationary (STAY shun airy) — not moving, fixed in place

synthetic (sin THET ick) — not of natural origin, manmade

technique (TECK NEEK) — the skill shown in a performance

vulnerable (VUL ner ah bul) — in a position to absorb possible injury

Further Reading

American Youth Soccer Organization, et. al. *The Official American Youth Soccer Handbook*. Fireside, 2001

Hornby, Hugh. *Soccer*. Dorling Kindersley, 2000

Quinn, Ron & Fleck, Tom. *Great Soccer Drills: The Baffled Parents' Guide*. Rugged Mountain Press, 2002

Websites to Visit

American Youth Soccer Association @ www.soccer.org/

Soccer Help @ www.soccerhelp.com

Soccer Times @ www.soccertimes.com

US Youth Soccer @ www.usysa.org/

Index

Association Football 7

backfielder 7

bicycle kick 13

corner kicks 29

dribbling 14-15, 17

football 4, 11

free kicks   28

goalkeeper 7, 24-27

kicking 10-13

midfielder 7

passing 17, 19, 22

penalty areas 6

penalty kicks 27, 28

referee 26

soccer ball 8

soccer field 6

striker 7, 13

trapping 21

About the Author

Morgan Hughes is the author of more than 50 books on hockey, track and field, bicycling, and many other subjects. He lives in Connecticut with his wife, daughter, and son.

DATE DUE

APR 1 7 2006		
SEP 1 1 2006		
OCT 1 7 2006		
NOV 0 9 2006		
NOV 3 0 2006		
JAN 2 2		
APR 0 5		
OCT 0 1 2007		
JAN		
MAR 0 6		
NOV 0		
NOV 1 4		
NOV 1 7		
OCT 1 6		
Oct 20 2014		